The Greenleaf Guide to Ancient Egypt

by Cynthia A. Shearer

Greenleaf Press
Lebanon, Tennessee

Voice (615)449-1617   FAX (615)449-4018
for orders only, call: 1-800-311-1508
Email: greenleafp@aol.com
World Wide Web Site: http://www.greenleafpress.com

3761 Highway 109 N., Unit D,
Lebanon, TN 37087
Phone: 615-449-1617

History for the thoughtful child

How To Use This Guide
Introduction:

When you want to build something, a hammer is a very useful thing to have. But if someone picks up your hammer and starts beating you over the head with it, the hammer is no longer a tool — it's a murder weapon. So it is with text books and study guides. This book is intended to be a tool, a possible model for you to use and adapt as you see fit. You will know what suggestions will work best for the students you teach. I hope you will find it useful.

Putting your study in context:

Before you begin your study of Ancient Egypt let me suggest that you put it in context — not so much chronological context as biblical context. Before our family began to study this material, we went back to the Old Testament and reviewed the first few chapters of Genesis and reread the descriptions of those who followed Adam and his sons. We made note of who were the farmers, who were herdsmen, who were workers in what craft. The picture that we saw there was very different from the typical evolutionary picture of Homo sapiens gradually leaving his primitive life as "hunter-gatherer" to settle down into more advanced stationary life-style. Read through to the story of the Tower of Babel. Discuss what you read together with the children you teach.

Once we had covered this material, we turned to the first chapter of Romans and read about what happens when man turns away from the truth and exchanges it for a lie. Again, we saw that the Bible paints a very different picture of the "evolution of religion" than that which is presented by evolutionary doctrines. Evolution teaches that man crawled out of the primordial mush a primitive animist. Our ancestors then gradually evolved to higher, more sophisticated forms of religion — becoming, first, polytheists and then monotheists (next step atheists?). The Bible, however, teaches just the opposite — that created man understood that there was one God, but as men turned away from God and rejected the truth, God turned them over to lies. Man exchanged the truth of monotheism for the lies of polytheism and animism.

As there has been something of a revival in the worship of female Egyptian deities (Isis, among others) in connection with the "New Age," witchcraft and "the worship of the goddess," I would recommend only a cursory study of Egyptian religion. The aim is to point to the differences between teachings of Egyptian religions and the teachings of the Bible, not to encourage a fascination with error.

However, some familiarity with Egyptian religion is necessary if we are to understand and appreciate what God did in Exodus. These were the gods that Moses challenged. And Moses and the Hebrews certainly knew enough about Egyptian religion to appreciate the pointed nature of the plagues. Each of the plagues was a direct challenge to specific objects of Egyptian worship. God's intent in each of the plagues was to show the Egyptian people (and the Hebrew people) that He alone was God, and beside Him there was no other. As Pharaoh claimed to be a god himself, the confrontations between Moses and Pharaoh can also be seen in this context. You might want to take this opportunity to review the Exodus together with your students as you begin your study of Ancient Egypt.

Suggestions for Teacher Preparation:

1. Familiarize yourself with the timeline at the back of the study guide, so that you have a sense of where you are going to begin and end. This will also briefly introduce you to the names of some of the people you will be reading about.

2. Read through the study guide's lessons and the assignments before you begin teaching them.

Methods of Evaluation:

When we think of testing, we usually think of exams — essay questions, true/false, multiple choice. There is a place for traditional testing both in and out of conventional classroom settings, but don't overlook the other options. If after reading a story, or listening to you read it aloud, the child is able to tell you the story in his own words — you can know that he understands it. That's really the reason for testing — to make sure your student understands the material.

Another means by which you can evaluate a student's understanding of a selection is through oral discussion. The "For Discussion" questions provided for each chapter are intended to be suggestions — questions you might ask. Often, as you discuss the reading, you will naturally cover the material without sticking to a rigid "question/answer" format. Treasure those times! Sometimes you will need to draw your students along point by point. Sometimes you will need to ask questions different from those suggested. By all means, do.

Written assignments also help evaluate understanding. Some "For Discussion" questions will work particularly well as essay topics. Occasionally have your students retell the story by presenting it as a news story, short story, play, etc.

Summary:

Our goals for the study of history are these:

1. That our students will see that God is involved in all history.
   Because God is involved in all of life, Scripture is relevant to all of life. Therefore, all things can and should be evaluated in light of Scripture. As we look at how men and women in our history have made choices, we have a unique opportunity to evaluate those choices as we see what kinds of endings they made for themselves. We can then consider what kind of lives we are building for ourselves and modeling for our children. In this way we can use history as a means by which God can teach us to number <u>our</u> days and apply <u>our</u> hearts to wisdom.

2. That when our students begin to study history in advanced courses they will not be starting from scratch, but will be building on a well-laid foundation.
   They will have a general knowledge of important people and events and have a good feel for what happened in what order. I do not expect a second grader to remember everything I teach about Egypt, for instance. But when he studies the material again later, he will find himself in familiar territory. Thus he will have to memorize less because he will have some familiarity with the people and places involved. In general, high school level history material is written in a way that assumes some prior knowledge of the stories. If you already know the basic facts about, say,

Charlemagne, you have less to memorize when you study him in high school. You can simply add the additional information to what you already know. (One of the things that makes history classes so boring is that very few students come to them with such a background. Because <u>everything</u> is new, <u>everything</u> must be memorized.)

Textbooks, by themselves, teach you facts. They do not introduce you to real people. Teaching history to elementary school students should be like calling a child to storytime. You find a snug comfortable place, you curl up together, and you start with "Once upon a time..."

Books Used in This Study:

This study guide makes use of the following books. As of this writing all are in print. Suggestions are made throughout the study that you look at various back issues of *National Geographic Magazine* and **National Geographic** videos.[1] You may know of others. Public Libraries may also have books that would be useful for supplemental reading. *The World Book Encyclopedia* is another excellent reference. However, the following six books will provide you with a solid base upon which to build your study of Ancient Egypt. The first two books will be used as primary texts. The remaining three expand on material mentioned in *The Pharaohs of Ancient Egypt*. (I have listed them, roughly, in order of sequence and frequency of use.)

Suggested Primary Texts:

Elizabeth Payne, *The Pharaohs of Ancient Egypt*, Random House (A Landmark Book) New York, 1964. This book is written for upper elementary aged children. If you are studying Egypt with older children, it is a good book to assign to them. If you are studying it with children who can not yet read the book independently, read it aloud to them. Like most of the Landmark Books, it covers the period pretty thoroughly in a way that is very accessible to children.

Tony Allan, *Time Traveller Book of Pharaohs and Pyramids*, Usborne Publishing Ltd., 1977. Excellent supplementary book. Colorful, informative pictures and captions. Places *The Pharaohs of Ancient Egypt* in an authentic visual setting.

Angela Wilkes, *Deserts*, Usborne Publishing Ltd., 1980.
   Arranged topically around such themes as location of deserts, life on the desert, animals and plant life, etc.

David Macaulay, *Pyramid*, Houghton Mifflin Company, Boston, 1975.
   Like the others in this series (*City, Castles*, and *Cathedrals*), this is a terrific book. Shows you how the pyramids were built, who built them, and why. It even shows you what tools they used. Don't study pyramids without it. (Just like *Castle* and *Cathedral*, there is a companion video to this volume — however, unlike *Castle* and *Cathedral* the video does not follow the book's story line as faithfully as the other two do. Parents should also be aware that one of the animation sequences contains a very brief bit of nudity as an Egyptian dancing girl turns slightly to the side.)

1 Note: The National Geographic folks generally base their material on belief in the myth of evolution, so do not expect the articles to speak with any final authority. (But then, you can always do what most people do anyway — enjoy the pictures and the maps).

Judy Donnelly, *Tut's Mummy — Lost... and Found*, Random House, New York, 1988. This is a book in the "STEP into Reading" series. It is written at the second to third grade reading level. Brightly illustrated with drawings and actual photographs of items found in the tomb.

Aliki Brandenberg, *Mummies Made in Egypt*, Harper Trophy, San Francisco, 1979. A "Reading Rainbow" book intended for ages 8 to 12. Like Aliki's other books, this one is rich in detailed information (and wonderful illustrations) showing how and why the Egyptians cared for their dead.

For Older Students: (grades 5-10)

Geraldine Harris, *Ancient Egypt*, Facts on File, New York, 1990. This is the first volume in the gorgeous *Cultural Atlas for Young People* series. Color photographs, rich detailed maps, and information about all aspects of life in Ancient Egypt. Independent Reading level is 7th grade and up. An especially useful book if you want to study Egypt with older students.

Historical Fiction:

Eloise Jarvis McGraw, *Mara, Daughter of the Nile*, Puffin Books, New York, 1953. A feisty slave girl finds herself playing the dangerous role of double agent for two arch enemies — each of whom supports a contender for the throne of Egypt. Reading level: junior high.

Eloise Jarvis McGraw, *The Golden Goblet*, Puffin Books, New York, 1961. A young boy is orphaned and left in the care of his older brother. His life's ambition has been to learn the trade of the goldsmith in whose shop he serves, but his brother threatens to apprentice him to the stone-cutters. And where does his brother get the money for his expensive clothes and habits? Reading level: upper elementary. A Newbery Honor book.

Games and Kits:

Catharine Roehrig, *Fun With Hieroglyphs*. A kit of 24 rubber stamps, an ink pad, and a key to the hieroglyph alphabet. Includes numerous activity ideas. Available from Greenleaf Press.

Make This Egyptian Temple, Usborne Publishing, Ltd. Includes obelisks and gateway, courtyard and hypostyle hall, sanctuary and priest's adjacent house on a 23x18 inch base, all covered with Egyptian art and hieroglyphs. Its OK, there's nothing weird or "new age." Available from Greenleaf Press.

Lesson One

The Geography of Egypt

1. Study a good relief map of Egypt.
   Locate any mountains, rivers, lakes, deserts.
   What are their names?

MOUNTAINS:	LAKES:
RIVERS:	**DESERTS:**
OCEANS/SEAS:	**OTHER:**

2. What major cities do you find?

_____

_____

_____

_____

3. Do the geographic features you listed divide the country into separated regions?

_____

_____

What features would provide natural defenses?

_____

_____

What areas of the country are more open to attack?

_____

_____

In what way?

_____

_____

_____

4. Where would you expect food to be grown most easily?

_____

_____

What other occupations would you expect to find in various regions of the country?

_____

_____

5. Take a piece of tracing paper and lay it over the relief map. Using a dark, soft lead pencil, trace the map of Egypt. Be sure to include and label major mountains, rivers, lakes, deserts, and cities. Note significant features bordering the areas you are studying.

6. Make a salt map which shows the major features of Egypt.

   Step 1: On an unbendable piece of cardboard (about 15 x 15 inches), draw the outline of Egypt. Be sure and use a pencil.

   Step 2: Make the salt/flour dough
   1 part salt
   2 parts flour
   Enough water to make a slightly sticky, but manageable dough.
   (1 cup salt, 2 cups flour will make enough dough for two good sized maps.)
   If you would like to color the dough to show differences in elevation or vegetation, add a little food coloring or tempera paint to the dough when you add the water.
   Be sure to use a bowl that won't be stained by the dye.

   Step 3: Take the salt dough and press it into the outline you have drawn on the cardboard. Build up ridges for mountains, make depressions in the dough to show rivers lakes or other low spots. You might want to use tempera paint to paint bordering oceans, nations, etc.

   Step 4: Lay map flat and let it dry overnight.

7. Find out more about deserts. Use **Desert**, a book in Usborne's First Traveller Series. Make use of an encyclopedia or **National Geographic Magazine** articles.

Lesson Two

How Do We Know What Ancient Egypt Was Like?

Texts:

The Pharaohs of Ancient Egypt, "The Rediscovery of Ancient Egypt," pages 3-19.

Time Traveller Book of Pharaohs, "How We Know About Ancient Egypt," page 30.

Vocabulary:

Note: The list of vocabulary words can be used in many ways, and indeed, its use should vary to fit the needs of individual students. If you are covering this material with an older child, you might want to select words from the list for use in spelling lessons. Choose an appropriate number for the week's work. Have the student copy them into a spelling notebook. You might have the child divide the words into syllables, learn the meanings of the words, and write sentences with them. For the younger child or the child who needs to follow a more systematic spelling program, skim the list for words that will need to be explained before the chapter is read. If you are reading the chapter aloud, you can generally just add a synonym or explanation as you read. Let the list be a help to you — something that you adapt to fit your own needs.

sweltering	frenzied	bleakly
catastrophe	campaign	vital
calamity	sultan	enfeebled
formidable	flicker	engraved
hieroglyph	curio	basalt
endure	excavation	lag
embedded	wracked	sheaf
deciphered	curiously	syntax
decipher	bogged down	concrete objects
abstract ideas	flourish	archaeology
archaeologist	spade	excavation
cartouches		

People and Places:

Rosetta

Rosetta Stone

Napoleon Bonapart

Mediterranean Sea

Nile River Delta

Major Pierre Bouchard

Ptolemy

Egyptian Expeditionary Force

Jean Francois Champollion

Assignment Options:

Read through this chapter and decide how you will use it. You might:

1. Assign it as independent reading to be discussed together after the students have read the material.

2. Read it aloud to the students, discussing it together as you read.

3. Use the material as reference material that you digest and narrate to your students. This option works well for younger students when you feel the material to be too dry, too technical, or too detailed to hold their attention. You can cover the material and liven it up where needed.

   For example, if your students are younger, you might summarize the material found in the above text and use the *Time Traveller Book of Pharaohs and Pyramids*, to illustrate main points:

   "How We Know About Ancient Egypt,"

   "How the Hieroglyphic Code was Cracked," page 30, and

   "Egyptian Writing,"

   "How to Read Hieroglyph," page 15.

   However, most of the chapters in *The Pharaohs of Ancient Egypt* are well suited to reading aloud.

Sample Summary of Information Contained in Chapter:

Though Egypt was once a great and mighty nation, by the time of Napoleon (the end of the 1700's) historians knew next to nothing about life in Ancient Egypt. There were references to Egypt's greatness in the Bible and in the writings of some Greek and Roman historians. The ruined Egyptian temples and the pyramids hinted at the richness of Egypt's past, but none of the details of its history were known.

To understand the life and history of an ancient culture, a historian needs to be able to read its writings and study archaeological evidence. In Napoleon's time, the science of archaeology was brand new, and no one knew how to read the Egyptian picture writings.

Napoleon was fascinated by Ancient Egypt and wanted to know more. He established the Egyptian Expeditionary Force. Its purpose was to invade the Nile Valley. As they invaded, they were to investigate the ruined temples, statues and pyramids, gathering information that would enable them to write a history of Ancient Egypt.

In 1799 Major Pierre Bouchard was supervising his troops as they dug trenches near the town of Rosetta. While his men were digging, they discovered a stone with messages in three different kinds of writing engraved upon it. One section was written in Greek, one in hieroglyphics, and one in an unrecognized language. The Stone, later to be called the Rosetta Stone, was sent to Alexandria with Napoleon's other curios.

As Napoleon's army moved through Egypt, a French artist named Dominique-Vivant Denon went along to investigate the Nile Valley. He made sketches of all he saw. When he returned to Cairo, he brought his sketch book with him and presented his findings to members of the Egyptian Institute. Though the members of the Institute were able to look at his sketches of the picture writing, they were not able to read it. This confirmed the fact that they needed to be able to read the hieroglyphics if they were ever going to make any progress in their study of Ancient Egypt. It was at this point that copies of the writings of the Rosetta Stone arrived.

Because the historians were able to read Greek they were able to determine that the message on the stone had been written in tribute to Pharaoh Ptolemy. They attempted to match the Greek text up with the hieroglyphics, but the symbols didn't match up. In 1822, Jean Francois Champollion noticed that Ptolemy's name appeared five times in the Greek section. He also noticed that there were five sets of circled drawings with identical sets of pictures. Thus he was able to identify the seven letters in Ptolemy's name. By filling in these seven known symbols wherever he found them in that section, he was able to decipher the name of another famous Egyptian leader, Cleopatra.[2]

Eventually, Champollion discovered that Egyptian symbols were of more than one type — there were twenty-four letter symbols standing for sounds in the Egyptian language **and** there were hundreds of signs that stood for both concrete objects and abstract ideas. Champollion was able to write an Egyptian grammar and dictionary. Taking Champollion's reference works and the copies of hieroglyphics made by various explorers, the code was cracked. Archaeologists, collectors and representatives from various museums poured into Egypt and the once-forgotten stories of Egypt's past were again known.

---

2 Because the process used here to decode the hieroglyphics is similar to the process used to decipher cryptograms, you might introduce your students to these coded puzzles. See puzzle included at end of this lesson.

Projects:

You might do a study of archaeology. Check your library for books on the subject. In conjunction with this, you might like to dig up a small plot of ground and bury some common household items — old cups (broken or whole), utensils, paper items, newspapers, magazine pages, toys (great place to hide an obnoxious toy!), things destined for the trash anyway. Leave them in the ground for a few months, then send your archaeologists out to excavate the ruins of this newly discovered site of a previously unknown ancient culture. Have them write descriptions of the "artifacts," including drawings of what they find. If there is broken pottery, let them attempt to glue it back together. What conclusions can they draw about this culture from their excavations? (Tongue in cheek, of course.)

For a short term version of this project, bury a variety of objects in the sandbox and let them excavate there. You could include the same writing assignments and have the same fun. Of course, you would not want to include any broken material in the sandbox.

Look at drawings of actual hieroglyphics. Check your library or an encyclopedia for material. *Hieroglyphics For Fun*, by Joseph and Lenore Scott (published by Van Nostrand in 1974) is one possible source. This book also contains a description of how to play the Egyptian game, Senet.
(See Lesson Nine of this study guide for details concerning the game.)

...CRYPTOGRAM — SECRET MESSAGE — CRYPTOGRAM...

A cryptogram is a coded message in which the letters you see in the message stand for other letters. When you know which letters stand for which, you can read the message. If X stands for a, that relationship will not change — anytime you see an X, you can count on the real letter being a. And in this puzzle, X **does** equal a all the way through the message. Have fun!

Record your findings here:

a	b	c	d	e	f	g	h	i	j	k	l	m
X												

n	o	p	q	r	s	t	u	v	w	x	y	z

SBNCGXQHX TXP FCQ PGNBBNA TOQE QEN BNQQNH S.

QEN NJWGQOXFP AOA FCQ VPN QEN BNQQNH S.

QEN NJWGQOXFP PGNBBNA SBNCGXQHX BOZN QEOP:

ZBNCGXQHX. JCQ OQ?

13

...CRYPTOGRAM — SECRET MESSAGE — CRYPTOGRAM...

Here are the answers:

a	b	c	d	e	f	g	h	i	j	k	l	m
X	R	S	A	N	M	J	E	O	K	Z	B	D

n	o	p	q	r	s	t	u	v	w	x	y	z
F	C	G	L	H	P	Q	V	I	T	U	W	Y

CLEOPATRA WAS NOT SPELLED WITH THE LETTER C.

THE EGYPTIANS DID NOT USE THE LETTER C.

THE EGYPTIANS SPELLED CLEOPATRA LIKE THIS:

KLEOPATRA. GOT IT?

For Discussion:

1. How was knowledge about the ancient Egyptians lost?

2. What was the Egyptian Expeditionary Force? Who organized it? From what country did its organizer come?

3. What was the Rosetta Stone? How was it found? What was on it? Why was the discovery of the Rosetta Stone significant? What effect did its discovery have on the study of Ancient Egypt?

4. Tell how Champollion was able to decipher the Rosetta Stone.

5. Tell what you know about hieroglyphics. How do hieroglyphics differ from the letters we use?

6. The poem "Ozymandias," by Percy Bysshe Shelley, tells the discovery of an ancient statue in the desert. Read the poem at least once out loud to yourself.

OZYMANDIAS

I met a traveler from an antique land
Who said: Two vast and trunkless legs of stone
Stand in the desert... Near them, on the sand,
Half sunk, a shattered visage lies, whose frown,
And wrinkled lip, and sneer of cold command,
Tell that its sculptor well those passions read
Which yet survive, stamped on these lifeless things,
The hand that mocked them, and the heart that fed:
And on the pedestal these words appear:
`My name is Ozymandias, king of kings:
Look on my works, ye Mighty, and despair!'
Nothing beside remains. Round the decay
Of that colossal wreck, boundless and bare
The lone and level sands stretch far away.

— Percy Bysshe Shelley

a. What was the inscription on Ozymandias' statue originally intended to mean? What message did it give to the traveler?

b. How did the message change? Can you see any similarities between the ruins of Ancient Egypt and the statue of Ozymandias?
(You might have your students memorize this poem)

Lesson Three

Unification of the Two Kingdoms and The Gift of the Nile

Texts:

The Pharaohs of Ancient Egypt, "The First Egyptians and the Dead Demigods," pages 20-39.

Note: pages 20 through most of page 24 are, at best, speculative. The author does say that there is much that archeologists do not know about the first people who lived in Egypt, but then she goes on to tell what probably happened. It is clear that she is writing from an evolutionary perspective. Read this section with <u>buckets</u> of salt. You may wish to frame your presentation of this bit of material with an appropriate, biblically based editorial comment or skip them altogether.

Time Traveller Book of Pharaohs and Pyramids, pages 6-7, 21, 26-27.

Peter Miller, "Riddle of the Pyramid Boats," *National Geographic Magazine*, April 1988 (Volume 173, No. 4), pages 534-550.

Robert Caputo, "Journey Up the Nile," *National Geographic Magazine*, May 1985, Volume 167, Number 5, pages 577-633. Includes detailed fold out map of the Nile.

Vocabulary:

swollen	churning	recede
desert scrub	silt	barren
tract	teem	gazelle
hyena	kemi	irrigation
engineering	skiff	chain reaction
papyrus	barter	dynasty
awesome		

People and Places:

The Red Land	The Black Land
Lower Egypt	The Nile
Nubia	Pharaoh Menes (also known as Narmer)
Manetho	

Chapter Outline:

1. "Hundreds and thousands of years... Oh My!" *The Pharaohs of Ancient Egypt*, pages 20-24.

2. Yearly flooding of the Nile, *The Pharaohs of Ancient Egypt*, pages 24-25.
   Supplemental Reading: *Time Traveller*, "Along the Nile," pages 6-7.

3. Irrigation, *The Pharaohs of Ancient Egypt*, pages 26-27.
   Activity: Build a model shaduf.

4. Transportation and Trade, *The Pharaohs of Ancient Egypt*, pages 27-28.
   Supplemental Reading: Peter Miller, "Riddle of the Pyramid Boats," *National Geographic Magazine*, April 1988 (Volume 173, No. 4), pages 534-550.

5. Unification of the Two Kingdoms, *The Pharaohs of Ancient Egypt*, pages 29-31.
   Supplemental Reading: *Time Traveller*, "Two Crowns," page 21.

6. Egyptian Belief in Life After Death, *The Pharaohs of Ancient Egypt*, pages 32-33.
   (includes a discussion of mummies and mummification, and how they were buried).
   Supplemental Reading: *Time Traveller*, "A Warrior is Buried," pages 26-27.

7. Egyptian Belief in the Deity of the Pharaoh, *The Pharaohs of Ancient Egypt*, pages 34-49.
   Supplemental Reading: *Time Traveller*, "At the Court of the Pharaoh," pages 20-21.

For Discussion:

1. Why did the Egyptians need to irrigate their fields?
   Find out what a shaduf was and how it was used.
   (See how to build a model shaduf on the following page. Decide whether you want to use this question as a research opportunity or dispense with the suspense and explain it to your students yourself.)
   Build a model of an Egyptian irrigation system.

2. How would the Ancient Egyptians have gotten from one place to another?
   Where do you think they would have most needed to go?
   What would have been the easiest mode of transportation?
   What materials would have been available to use for boat building?

3. On a map, show the location of the original two kingdoms of Egypt. Tell how they became united into one nation.

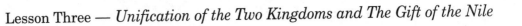

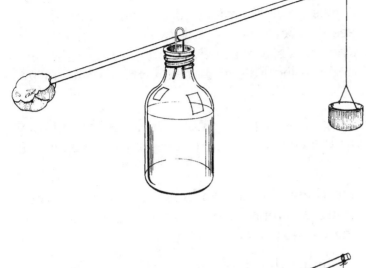

There are two ways to make a model shaduf. You can use an empty bottle (2L or 16oz plastic work well). The bottle cap works well for the water bucket. Use a small dowel for the long lever, with a ball of non-hardening modeling clay for the weight

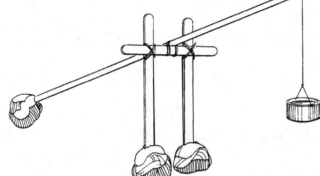

You can also build a goal-post style shaduf using three popsicle sticks for the goal. Some more of the non-hardening modeling clay will work to support the goalposts.

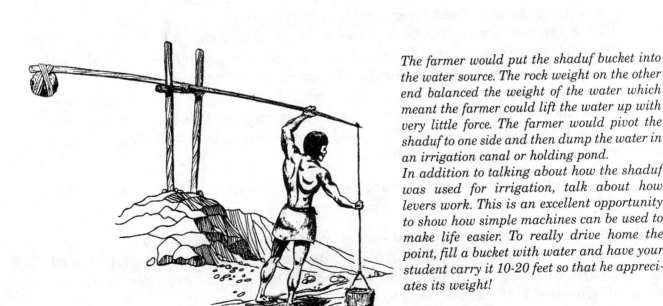

The farmer would put the shaduf bucket into the water source. The rock weight on the other end balanced the weight of the water which meant the farmer could lift the water up with very little force. The farmer would pivot the shaduf to one side and then dump the water in an irrigation canal or holding pond.

In addition to talking about how the shaduf was used for irrigation, talk about how levers work. This is an excellent opportunity to show how simple machines can be used to make life easier. To really drive home the point, fill a bucket with water and have your student carry it 10-20 feet so that he appreciates its weight!

4. What did the Egyptians believe happened to them after death?

Note: Be careful not to confuse the ancient Egyptians with — the Frisbee-terians, who believe that when you die your soul goes up on the roof and you can't get it down... (just kidding, we were checking to see if everyone was still awake... hee hee!) You will cover this in more depth when you study the Pyramids in Lesson Five. Touch it lightly here, or read ahead to Lesson Five and decide whether or not to cover it in depth at this point.

5. Describe the Egyptians' understanding of their place in the world. What did they believe about their relationship with the gods and with other nations? Whom did they call foreigners?

6. What did the Egyptians believe about their Pharaoh and his relationship to the gods? As a god himself, what was Pharaoh supposed to be able to do for his people? What were some of the things he was expected to do?

7. When Moses stood before Pharaoh claiming that the Almighty God had sent him with a message for Pharaoh, why would you expect Pharaoh to respond in a hostile manner? What point was God trying to make to all of Egypt (and to the Hebrews)?

Related Study:

1. Now would be a good time to begin a study of simple machines for science (e.g. levers, wheels, pulleys, inclined planes). With the next lesson, you begin a study of the pyramids and the tools used to build them which will provide a number of examples of simple machines. If you build a model shaduf, you have a wonderful opportunity to talk about levers and how they work.
Check your science textbooks for ideas. One possibility would be the Science in a Nutshell kit called "Work, Plane and Simple" ($32.98, available from Greenleaf Press). Our Merrill's third grade *Accent on Science* textbook covered it simply and cheaply and was even fun. Or check your favorite School Supply Store for unit-study-style kits on simple machines. They range in price from $11.00 for "How Things Work," from the Backyard Science series, to $39.95 for Educational Insights, "Science in Action" kit.

2. You could study the history of paper — its more exciting than it sounds (a little more anyway). You could make your own paper.

3. You could also learn to weave a basket. Would reeds have been good weaving material? Inexpensive basket weaving kits are available from Nasco *Arts and Crafts Catalog*. Write them care of Nasco, 901 Janesville Ave., Fort Atkinson, Wisconsin 53538, (414) 563-2446.

Lesson Four

Pharaoh Cheops and the Great Pyramid

Texts:

The Pharaohs of Ancient Egypt, pages 40-63.

Time Traveller Book of Pharaohs and Pyramids:
      "Along the Nile," pages 6-7,
      "At Home with Nakht," pages 8-9,
      "Giving a Feast," pages 10-11,
      "Visit to a Temple," pages 12-13,
      "A Warrior is Buried," pages 24-25.

Vocabulary:

proportioned
beacon
inlaid
commandeered
causeway
eerie
skiff
hippopotamus
fowling skiff
cargo
furled
teemed
scribe
personified
gauzy
conceive
conscripted
desecration

mute
sarcophagus
awe
oppression
detest
juncture
ward off
skittered
import
enable
kilts
relish (v.)
transaction
absorb
imposing
sheathed
apex

capstone
ebony
compel
conveyance
pinnacle
perishable
crocodile
maneuvered
stevedores
prevailing winds
exquisite
flax
bustling
essence
visier
idleness
block and tackle

People and Places:

Herodotus
Memphis
mastaba tombs
Imhotep
Egyptologist

The Great Pyramid of Giza
Royal Precinct
Pharaoh Zoser
the Inundation

Chapter Outline:

1. Ancient Greek historian, Herodotus and the Great Pyramid, ***The Pharaohs of Ancient Egypt***, pages 40-44.

2. Modern Archaeologists and the Great Pyramid, ***The Pharaohs of Ancient Egypt***, pages 44-45.

3. Pharaoh Cheops — His Daily Life and Duties, ***The Pharaohs of Ancient Egypt***, pages 46-52.

4. Building Pyramids, ***The Pharaohs of Ancient Egypt***, pages 53-62.
   (You will need to decide whether you want to read this section first, treating it as a general introduction to the building of pyramids and follow it with the study of Macaulay's ***Pyramid***, or go straight on to ***Pyramid*** and skip this section. The other alternative is to skip Macaulay, but his book is so good, I hate to even suggest that.)

For Discussion:

1. Compare what Herodotus was told about Cheops with information found by Egyptologists. Which view do you think is likely to be more accurate? Why?

2. Describe life in Memphis.

Lesson Five
Pyramids and Life After Death

Texts:

Pyramid

Time Traveller Book of Pharaohs and Pyramids,
"A Warrior is Buried," and "The World of the Spirits," pages 24-27.
"Visit to a Temple," pages 12-13.

Background Information:

Note: See the discussion on pages 1 & 2 about the study of Egyptian religion.

Vocabulary:

(See the glossary in the back of the book for a list of the more technical vocabulary.)

coronation	supremacy	plateau
decree	compensate	complex (noun)
mortuary	portcullis	inscribe
enormous	incense	hoisted
embalm	oblong	funerary
simultaneously	mason	mortar
quarry	horizon	expose
limestone	ferry	sarcophagus
capstone	dismantle	mummy
embalmer	caverns	lever
embedded	accurate	oriented
horizon	surveyor	dock
causeway	friction	protrude
erect (verb)	mummified	elaborate

People and Places:

Hall of the Two Truths	Books of the Dead
Osiris	Meresger
Anubis	Devourer
Thoth	Horus
Fields of Yaru	

For Discussion:

1. Consider making a model of a pyramid. Use sugar cubes and white glue, legos, blocks, whatever is plentiful and handy. OR Draw a map of a typical pyramid.

2. Why were the pyramids built?

3. What did Egyptians believe happened to the pharaoh after he died? Explain why the burial chambers were filled with everyday objects and elaborate treasures. What does the Bible tell us about what happens to a person after his or her death?

4. Read Romans 14: 8-12 (. . . For we shall all stand before the judgment seat of Christ...) and I Corinthians 3:9-23. Compare it with the journey of the soul to the Hall of the Two Truths.
   What did the Egyptians rely on for salvation? What did they believe was the basis of judgment? How does that compare with the teaching of Scripture? Support your answer with specific Scripture.

Lesson Six

"I Show Thee a Land Topsy-Turvy"

Texts:

Time Traveller Book of Pharaohs and Pyramids, "The Story of the Pharaohs," page 28, and "Going to School," page 14.

Pharaohs of Ancient Egypt, pages 64-79.

Read with or assign to your students: *Time Traveller Book of Pharaohs and Pyramids*, page 28, for an overview of the material covered in this chapter of *Pharaohs of Ancient Egypt*.

In this chapter you will also read about ancient scrolls containing the day to day records of an Egyptian estate. For background information on how Egyptian scribes were schooled and how the scrolls were made, read "Going to School" on page 14 of *The Time Traveller Book*.

Period Summary:

2200-2050 FIRST INTERMEDIATE PERIOD

Dynasties Seven through Eleven

This period is characterized by civil war; fighting between nobles for control of power. As might be expected, Egypt experienced a decline in trade during this time. Discomfort with absolutist kings, there was a greater concern for justice during this period than before. It was during this time that the priests decreed that those without royal ancestry could indeed be admitted to heaven. Osiris, who was already a major deity, was designated as the ruler of the dead.

2050-1800 MIDDLE KINGDOM — EGYPTIAN EMPIRE
Twelfth Dynasty

> 1898 B.C. Joseph sold into slavery
>
> 1885 B.C. Joseph made second in command
>
> 1878 B.C. Seven year famine
>
> 1876 B.C. Jacob and family move to Egypt
>
> 1805 B.C. Death of Joseph

Theban nobles won out over the other families and ruled Egypt. By the end of the period, the kings had regained their lost powers.

1800-1570 - SECOND INTERMEDIATE PERIOD
Dynasties Thirteen through Seventeen

Characterized by weak rulers. Local princes regain some of their former independence.

1730-1570 Period of Hyksos Invasion and Influence

Hoard sweeps in from Asia with horses and chariots. They introduce body armor and bronze weapons. Dominate Egypt for 160 years.

1570-1300 EARLY NEW KINGDOM
Eighteenth Dynasty

The Egyptian people learned from the Hyksos how to use weapons and in 1570, drove them back into Asia.

Chapter Outline:

1. At the end of the last century, thieves discovered day-to-day records kept by an overseer of country estate soon after the death of Cheops, ***The Pharaohs of Ancient Egypt***, pages 64-68.

2. What the records tell about the 1000 year period following Cheops death and the nobles revolt; Theban prince restores order; nobles revolt; Theban leader Amenemhet seizes throne; Hyksos invade; Hyksos driven out, ***The Pharaohs of Ancient Egypt***, pages 68-79.

Vocabulary:

exploits	fortresses	frontiers
summon	antiquities	apathetic
black-market	smuggle	parley
votive offerings	overseer	invaluable
rubbish	jubilant	squalor
anarchy	defy	allotted
revenge	subdued	filtered
obscure	ruthless	horde
vile	wretched	subservient
imposing	pleated	

People and Places:

Giza	Old Kingdom	Middle Kingdom
Nubia	Hyksos	Amon
Pharaoh Amenemhet	Syria	Ahmose
Thutmose	ka	

For Discussion:

1. What change in religious belief about the afterlife affected the building of the pyramids?

2. What had the invasion of the Hyksos taught the Egyptians about their nation's defenses? What affect did this have on their foreign policies?

3. Compare Pharaoh Cheops with the Pharaohs that followed him.
   How did Pharaoh Cheops' subjects seem to feel about him?
   How did they seem to feel about his successors?

4. In what way could Egypt have been described as a "land topsy-turvy?"

5. Who were the Hyksos? Where did they come from?
   What did they do? How long did they stay?

6. Describe life under Thutmose I. Compare it to life under Cheops.

Student_____ Date_____

READING ASSIGNMENT CHART

Topic _____

Book Titles:

    (1) _____

    (2) _____

    (3) _____

Date	Book/Chapter	Pages

Copy as many of these as you need as you plan your study.

Lesson Seven
Queen Hatshepsut

Text:

The Pharaohs of Ancient Egypt, "'His Majesty, Herself' — Queen Hatshepsut,"
   pages 80-96.

Time Traveller Book of Pharaohs and Pyramids, "The Story of the Pharaohs," page
   29. (This section provides an overview of the Pharaohs from Hatshepsut onward.)

> "Hatshepsut may have been the royal princess who dis-
> covered Moses along the Nile... During Hatshepsut's
> brilliant reign Egypt experienced prosperity. In these
> years Moses spent his youth in the royal court."
> ***The Bible Knowledge Commentary***, **page 106.**

Vocabulary:

terraces	fragrant	sphinxes
mutilated	presumably	tangle
harem	Dowager	regent
theoretically	deferred	don
coup d'etat	ambition	entanglements
barbaric	conquest	vested interest
depose	seethe	banish
vizier	marvel	dais
partisans	prostrated	unassailable
audacity	dissident	infuriate
obelisk	electrum	enmity
intrigue	interlude	virtual prisoner
obliterated		

People and Places:

Queen Hatshepsut	Deir el Bahri
Senmut	Punt
Thutmose II	

For Discussion:

1. Tell how Hatshepsut became Queen of Egypt. Who was her husband? Why was this man chosen for her?

2. How many children did Hatshepsut and Thutmose II have? Hatshepsut had no male children, but Thutmose II did. Explain this.

3. Why did Thutmose II marry his young daughter to his "secondary wife's" son?

4. When Thutmose II died, who became the new Pharaoh?
    Who became the new Queen of Egypt?
    What did Hatshepsut become?

5. How content was Hatshepsut with this arrangement? What did she do about it?

6. Describe Hatshepsut's foreign policy. Contrast it with the foreign policy of her father.

7. What did Hatshepsut do with Thutmose III?

8. Who was Senmut? What was his relationship with Hatshepsut?

9. Tell about Hatshepsut's expedition to Punt. Why did they go? What did they do? How were they received? What did the Egyptians think of the voyage?

10. Tell how the priests loyal to Thutmose III express their feelings about Hatshepsut's reign?
    What was Hatshepsut's response?

11. After Hatshepsut's death, Thutmose III returned to the throne. How did he honor Hatshepsut's memory? If *The Bible Knowledge Commentary* is correct, and Moses was living in the court during Hatshepsut's reign, how do you think Thutmose III would have felt about him?

Thutmose the Third

Texts:

The Pharaohs of Ancient Egypt, "The Smiter of the Asiatics — Pharaoh Thutmose the Third," pages 97-118.

Time Traveller Book of Pharaohs and Pyramids, "Battle," pages 22-23.

Chapter Outline:

1. Pharaoh Thutmose III comes to power. Restores Egypt to major power in the region, ***The Pharaohs of Ancient Egypt***, pages 97-111.

2. How Thutmose's mummy was found, ***The Pharaohs of Ancient Egypt***, pages 111-118.

Vocabulary:

smite	recruit	sprawling
javelins	advance scouts	lumbering
encamped	ambush	vanguard
oblige	massed	ramparts
untidy	formidable	resplendent
pavilion	absurdity	paralyzed
pandemonium	barricade	retainers
recourse	humiliation	booty
dumbfounded	hostage	swarthy
manacled	distaste	tribute
extensive	garrisons	ambassadors
vassals	reputation	retinue
precincts	exotic	isolation
disheveled	cache	riveted
afrit	despoiling	straggle

People and Places:

Carmel Mountains	Megiddo
Abderrassul	Emile Brugsch

The Pharaoh of the Exodus

"Thutmose III was succeeded by Amenhotep II (1450-1425), the Pharaoh of the Exodus (1446). Unlike his warring father, Amenhotep II seems to have suffered military reverses because he was not able to carry out extensive campaigns. His weak war efforts may have resulted from the loss of all or most of his chariots, in the waters of the Sea of Reeds. The so called "Dream Stela" of Thutmose IV records that the god Harem-akht told the young prince in a dream that he would be king. If Thutmose IV had been the eldest son, proof of his throne-right would have been unnecessary. It is logical, therefore, to assume that he was the younger son, not the oldest son of Amenhotep II. This accords with the statement of Exodus 12:29 that the eldest son of Pharaoh died the night of Israel's first Passover.

"Thus Thutmose III was the Pharaoh of the oppression and Amenhotep II was the Pharaoh of the Exodus."

The Bible Knowledge Commentary, pages 106-107.

For Discussion:

1. Compare and Contrast Hatshepsut and Thutmose III.
   What was each like? How did their foreign policies differ?

2. Describe the Battle of Megiddo. How did the Egyptian soldiers miss a valuable opportunity to take the city?
   How was the city eventually taken?

3. Pretend you are standing in the crowd at Thebes. You watch the parade of returning troops and captives. What do you see, hear, and think? Write a story in which you record your impressions. You might record a conversation that you might have had with a friend during the parade. You might write a pretend journal entry (in your papyrus journal, of course!). Use your imagination.

4. Where did Thutmose III go every spring? Why?
   Find the boundaries of his kingdom on a map.

5. How did Thutmose III "Egyptianize" the governments of surrounding lands? How did this policy work to his advantage?

6. What was life like when Thutmose III returned to Egypt every fall? How did he spend his winters?

7. Who succeeded Thutmose III after his death?

8. Tell how Thutmose III's remains were found.

9. If you were an Israelite living in Thutmose III's Egypt, what would life have been like for you? Be specific.

At this point, re-read the account of the Exodus found in Exodus 4:18-15:1-21. (See "Dating the Exodus" found in the timeline at the end of this study guide for information concerning the controversy over the dating of this event.)

Each of the Ten Plagues of the Exodus represented a direct attack on specific Egyptian gods and goddesses. When I read the story of the Exodus as a child, it always seemed to me that God was really picking on the Egyptian people. It seemed to me as though God got up each morning, looked at Gabriel and (sort of the same way T.V. game show hosts asked their announcers about the prizes of the day) said, "Well Gabe, what do we have for these fine people today." I knew that God was just, but that was all I had to temper my impression of the plagues. When I understood that each time God plagued the Egyptians, he was demonstrating his authority over the many false gods of the Egyptians, it opened up a whole new world to me. The Egyptians and Israelites knew exactly which gods were being challenged. Our children need to understand this, too.

Go over the following material with your students, discussing it with them as you read through the story of the Exodus. We covered about one plague a day. As we would begin the story of a new plague, we would try to remember the previous plagues from memory. To help in this we came up with this rhyme:

> Blood, frogs,
> gnats and flies
> Cattle died.
> Boils, hail,
> locust, dark
> Egypt wails
> Israel departs.

According to *The Bible Knowledge Commentary: An Exposition by Dallas Seminary Faculty*, edited by John F. Walvoord and Roy B. Zuck, each of the plagues were associated with the specific Egyptian deities as follows:

The Nile turned to Blood	Hapi, god of the Nile Isis, goddess of the Nile Khnum, guardian of the Nile
Frogs	Heqet, goddess of birth (usually depicted with the head of a frog)
Lice ~~Gnats~~	Set, the god of the desert
Flies	Re, the sun god, his symbol may have been the fly
Death of Livestock	Hathor, goddess with cow's head Apis, the bull god, also a fertility symbol
Boils	Sekhmet, had power over diseases Sunu, god of pestilence Isis, goddess of healing
Hail	Nut, goddess of the sky Osiris, god of crops and fertility Set, god of storms
Locusts	Nut, goddess of the sky Osiris, god of crops and fertility
Darkness	Re, the sun god Horus, the sun god Nut, goddess of the sky Hathor, sky goddess
Death of Firstborn	Min, god of reproduction Hequet, goddess associated with childbirth Isis, goddess protecting children Pharaoh's firstborn son, a god, himself

Lesson Nine

Pharaoh Akhnaton (The Monotheistic Pharaoh) and Pharaoh Tutankhamon

<u>Texts:</u>
The Pharaohs of Ancient Egypt, pages 119-152.

Time Traveller Book of Pharaohs and Pyramids, "At the Court of the Pharaoh," pages 20-21.
As you read about Amenhotep III in *Pharaohs of Ancient Egypt*, read "Archaeological Triumph — Tutankhamen's Tomb," page 31.

Tut's Mummy — Lost and Found, 46 pages. (This is a book in the Random House "STEP into Reading" series. It is written at the second to third grade reading level.)

Chapter Outline:

1. An Arab peasant woman finds Babylonian cuneiform tablets that tell Akhnaton's story, *The Pharaohs of Ancient Egypt*, page 119-122.

2. Amenhotep III, *The Pharaohs of Ancient Egypt*, pages 122-125.

3. Amenhotep IV and Nefertiti, *The Pharaohs of Ancient Egypt*, pages 125-126.

4. The rise of Aton — Amenhotep changes his name to Akhn**aton**, forsakes worship of other gods, moves capital. Political opposition eventually restores Amon to prominence. Death of Akhnaton.

5. Tutankh**aton** becomes Tutankh**amon**, *The Pharaohs of Ancient Egypt*, pages 143-147.

6. Discovery of Tutankhamon's unspoiled tomb, *The Pharaohs of Ancient Egypt*, pages 147-152.

Vocabulary:

sebkh	nitrous	gunny sack
cuneiform	papyrus	genuine
forged	interlude	fanatic
impassable	gape	din
courtiers	glandular disorder	moody
unassailable	curb	cosmopolitan
homage	devotee	implacable foe
ungainly	terse	profusion
death knell	revert	flotilla
blight	ankh	rudimentary
perspective	dandling	lax
profusion	heretic	detest

People and Places:

Tell el Amarna	Amenhotep III	Queen Tiy
Amenhotep IV	Nefertiti	Karnak
Aton	Akhnaton	Haremhab
Howard Carter	Lord Carnarvon	

For Discussion:

1. How long after the death of Thutmose III did Amenhotep III come to rule? What was Egypt like under him?

2. Describe Amenhotep III's relationship with the High Priest of Amon.

3. Tell about the rise of the worship of Aton. How was Aton different from Ra, the sun god?
   (Whereas Ra was traditionally worshipped as the god of the sun, Aton was one step above that — Aton was the name given to the sun's very orb.)

4. How did Amenhotep IV's (remember, he changed his name to Akhnaton) foreign policies compare with his father's foreign policy? How did these differences eventually contribute to Amenhotep IV's downfall?

5. What was the relationship between Akhnaton and Amenhotep IV?
   (If you said that those are just two names for the same person, you are right.) How did Amenhotep IV come to change his name? What is the meaning of each name?

6. What was Akhnaton's attitude toward the other Egyptian dieties? How did he show this? How were his actions received? At what point did Akhnaton really "go too far," according to those around him?

7. Describe life in the city of Akhetaton? What was different about the way Akhnaton conducted himself? What did his relationship with his family appear to be like?

8. What differences can be seen between the art of his time and art of earlier and later times? What instructions did Aknaton give his artists? Why do you think he did this?
   Which style do you like better?

9. Tell how Akhnaton came to leave the city of Akhetaton.

What seems to have happened?

10. After Akhnaton's death, what did Nefertiti do, perhaps in an effort to preserve the worship of Aton? What was the new Pharaoh's name?

11. After Pharaoh Tutankamon's death, what happened to the city of Akhetaton and the memory of Akhnaton?

12. Tutankamon was not a very important Pharaoh. Why is he so well known today?

13. Read **Tut's Mummy — Lost... and Found**, by Judy Donnelly.
    For instructions on how to play the game that was found in Tut's tomb, — pictured on page 7 of **Tut's Mummy — Lost and Found** — see the next page of this study guide.

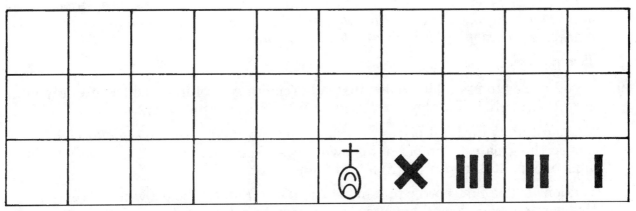

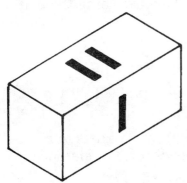

The rolling stick has four sides, number one through four. There are no numbers on the end.

Each player needs ten (10) markers. The two sets of markers should be of contrasting colors or design. The markers are set up on the top two rows of the board in alternating fashion, thus:

X O X O X O X O X O

O X O X O X O X O X

The Game of Senet

Rules of Play:

1. Roll the rolling stick and move the number of spaces indicated. Players alternate, making one move each turn.

2. You must move your piece toward the marks at the bottom right-hand corner of the board.
    You must move your piece either up, down or from left to right.
    You may NOT move backwards or diagonally.
    You may move in a straight line, OR turn a corner, OR do both, but you must always move your piece toward the marks at the bottom right-hand end of the board.

3. Your playing piece must land on either an empty spot or on a space occupied by your opponent.
    If you land on your opponent's square, that piece is captured and removed from the board.
    If your only move would force you to land on a square occupied by your own piece, you may not move.
    If you cannot use the number rolled, you lose that turn.

4. No piece may be captured once it rests on one of the board's five marked squares, but you may not let your piece just sit there. If it is possible to move a piece on a marked square then that move MUST be made.
    To move a piece off the board, you must roll the exact number needed. If you are on square III, you must roll a 3 to take it from the board.
    If the player is on the III square and rolls a 1 or a 2, and those spaces are open, he must take that move. Only if the roll cannot be used for one of the pieces on marked squares may he move another of his pieces.

5. Two pieces cannot occupy the same space.

6. If you prefer to use a single die, instead of making a rolling stick, count only numbers 1 through 4. If a player rolls a 5 or a 6, he loses that turn.

7. Version I: Play until all pieces are removed from the board. The player who has moved the greatest number of his own pieces from the board wins. Pieces lost to your opponent or captured from him do not count.

    Version II: The first player to remove one piece from the board wins. If you play this version, players will have to try to prevent each other from reaching the end of the board.
    Cut-throat Senet, anyone?

NOTE: The mark ☥ represents the Egyptians letters "nfr" and stood for the word, "good." Once your piece reaches or passes this mark it is safe from capture. X represents the number 4 and III, II, and I mean 3, 2, and 1.

The hieroglyph for the biliteral "mn" ▭ is thought by many Egyptologists to represent a senet game . It also stood for the word "remain" which appears to be a reference to the strategy for playing senet.

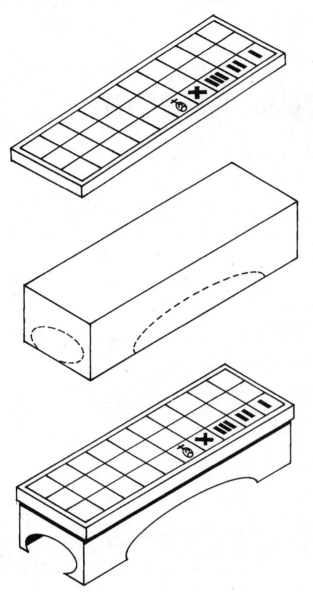

Make a Model
of Tut's Senet Game

You will need:
a copy of the Senet board found on page 51
of this guide

a shoebox and lid

scissors and glue

First Step: Paste the cutout copy of the Senet board on top of the shoebox lid.

Second Step: Turn the shoebox over and cut out the sections as shown at left on all four sides.

Step Three: Glue the lid to the bottom of the shoebox as shown at left. Decorate the box as you like.

For hints on decoration and appearance, see the picture of Tut's Senet game on page 7 of <u>Tut's Mummy... Lost and Found</u>.

Student _____ Date _____

READING ASSIGNMENT CHART

Topic _____

Book Titles:

    (1) _____

    (2) _____

    (3) _____

Date	Book/Chapter	Pages

Copy as many of these as you need as you plan your study.

Lesson Ten

Pharaoh Rameses the Second

Text:

The Pharaohs of Ancient Egypt, "The Beginning of the End — Pharaoh Rameses the
Second," pages 153-172.

For information on the discovery of the ships mentioned at the end of the chapter, read
the following article: Farouk El-Baz, "Finding Pharaoh's Funeral Bark," **National
Geographic Magazine**, (April 1988, Volume 173, No. 4) page 513-533.

Chapter Outline:

1. Rameses II, **The Pharaohs of Ancient Egypt**, pages 153-164.

2. Egypt's Decline — Invasions -Floods, famines and weak kings, **The Pharaohs of
Ancient Egypt**, pages 165-170.

3. Alexander the Great, Ptolemy and Rome, **The Pharaohs of Ancient Egypt**,
pages 170-172

Vocabulary:

disintegrated	penetrating	loping
armaments	rendezvous	inexplicable
stupendous	repelled	depict
steles	egoist	retinue
painstaking	dowry	appropriating

People and Places:

Kadesh	Rameses II	Orontes
Mutuwallis	Aleppo	Tanis
Battle of Kadesh	Hypostyle Hall	Abu Simbel
Tigris Euphrates	Tiber River	Alexander the Great
Alexandria	Ptolemy	Cleopatra
Mohammed		

For Discussion:

1. Describe the coronation of Rameses II.

2. What parts of the lands formerly a part of the Egyptian Empire were still held by Egypt when Rameses II came to power? What people watched and waited as Rameses II began to rebuild the Empire?

3. Tell about the Battle of Kadesh. Who fought? How were the Egyptian Army divisions named? Describe the ambush. How did Mutuwallis' spies lure Rameses II into the ambush? What was the result of the ambush? How did Rameses II manage to get out of the battle alive?

4. Contrast the truth of the battle with Rameses II's report of the battle. If you had been at the battle, survived it and returned to Thebes — would you have recognized the battle from Rameses II's version of it?

5. What would you find at the temple of Abu Simbel?

6. How would you describe Rameses II?

7. In the period after the death of Rameses III, what things happened that made Egypt even more vulnerable to attack and or decline? Describe life during this period.

8. Briefly tell about the nations that ruled over Egypt after the nation declined.

Timeline Of Egyptian History

Biblical Dates & Egyptian Dates

There is a great deal of controversy about the earliest dates in Egyptian history. Many feel that the Egyptian chronicles which list pharaohs going back to 5000 B.C. are pure fabrication. The earliest Egyptian dates conflict with traditional biblical dating - if you take the world-wide scope of the flood seriously. The flood is traditionally dated in 2348 B.C. After this date came the building of the tower of Babel and the dispersion of Noah's descendants in 2247 B.C. After these events, the rise of a kingdom in Egypt is consistent with biblical accounts. Another way to reconcile the two dating systems is to suppose that the Biblical events of the flood and Tower of Babel occurred much earlier, and therefore prior to, the rise of the Egyptian civilization.

5000 B.C.[3]	Egypt's Two Kingdoms
3200	Unification of Two Kingdoms Pharaoh Menes
2686-2181	The Old Kingdom (**Note** that at this point it was generally accepted that only pharaohs could expect to be accepted into heaven)

First Intermediate Period

2200-2050

Dynasties Seven through Eleven

This period was characterized by civil war — fighting between nobles for control of power. As might be expected, Egypt experienced a decline in trade during this time. Discomfort with absolutist pharaohs may have led to the development of greater concern for justice during this period than before. It was during this time that the priests decreed that those without royal ancestry could indeed be admitted to heaven. Osiris, who was already a major deity, was designated as the ruler of the dead.

Middle Kingdom — Egyptian Empire

2050-1800

Twelfth Dynasty

Theban nobles won out over the other competing families and ruled Egypt. By the end of the period, the kings had regained their lost powers.

1898 B.C.	Joseph sold into slavery
1885 B.C.	Joseph made second in command
1878 B.C.	Seven year famine
1876 B.C.	Jacob and family move to Egypt

[3] All dates in the timeline are B.C. unless noted otherwise.

| 1805 B.C. | Death of Joseph |

1800-1570 Second Intermediate Period
Dynasties Thirteen through Seventeen
Characterized by weak rulers. Local princes regain some of their former independence.

1730-1570 Period of Hyksos Invasion and Influence
Hoard sweeps in from Asia with horses and chariots. They introduce body armor and bronze weapons. Dominate Egypt for 160 years.

1570-1300 Early New Kingdom

Eighteenth Dynasty

The Egyptian people learned from the Hyksos how to use weapons and in 1570, drove them back into Asia.

Thutmose I - Strong central government

Queen Hatshepsut (1505-1484) - Focus of reign on internal matters. Built temples and palaces. Launched large trade expedition to parts of Africa. Ruled jointly with Thutmose II for a time. (Queen Hatshepsut may have been the princess who pulled the infant Moses from the river.)

Thutmose III (1484-1461) - Focused on extension of Egypt's boundaries. His empire lasted 100 years, making Thebes and Memphis the political, cultural, and commercial center of the world. (Believed to have been the Pharaoh who oppressed the children of Israel.)

Dating the Exodus

There are two Pharaohs most often associated with the Exodus: Amenhotep II and Ramses II.

According to *The Bible Knowledge Commentary: An Expositon by Dallas Seminary Faculty*, edited by John F. Walvoord and Roy B. Zuck, an earlier dating of the Exodus (c. 1453 BC) during the reign of Amenhotep II is more consistent with the Biblical record and archeological findings than is the later dating (c. 1250 BC), which would make Rameses II the Pharaoh in question. See *The Bible Knowledge Commentary* or the very useful series of charts in *Chronological and Background Charts for the Old Testament* for the details of the controversy. If the Exodus occurred in 1453 BC, then Akhnaton, (whose name had originally been Amenhotep IV) Egypt's monotheistic pharaoh, would have ruled approximately 60 years after the Exodus.

Recently, a maverick Egyptologist, David Rohl, has proposed a radically different chronology for Egyptian history. His re-dating of the reigns of the Pharaohs places Amenhotep II and Ramses much later than traditional chronologies - well after either 1453 BC or 1250 BC (the two candidates for the date of the Exodus). Rohl's chronology would make Akhnaton a contemporary of King Saul and King David. See *Pharaohs and Kings: A Biblical Quest* for more details.

Amenhotep II (1450-1425) - Official Greenleaf Press choice for "Pharaoh of the Exodus."

Amenhotep IV (1361-1344) - Changed his name to Akhenaton in honor of the god he called the One True God, Aton. Married to Nefertiti. He moved the capital from Thebes, which was the center of the old religion, to Akhetaton 300 miles to the north. Outlying possessions are lost and Egypt's boundaries shrink. During this period the title, "Pharaoh," comes into use.

Tutankhamon (1341-1332) - succeeded Akhenaton, returned to old religion. Thebes restored as the capital.

1300-1090   **Later New Kingdom — "The Golden Age"**

Nineteenth and Twentieth Dynasties

During this time Egypt recovered its empire in Asia, as well as its leading position in trade and commerce. Egypt battled the Hittites from Asia and the Philistines from the eastern Mediterranean.

Haremhab died without heirs. Kingdom passes to his vizier Rameses. Rameses' son is Seti. Seti's son is Rameses II.

Ramses II (1291-1224) - Alternate choice for "Pharaoh of the Exodus."

Battle of Kadesh — Rameses II takes on the Hittites

By 1150 Egypt was having difficulty competing with the nations who had access to iron, and thus had iron weapons. Egypt lost its outlying possessions and was then divided into small states that cooperated in matters of trade and commerce, but competed politically.

1090-945   **Post Empire Period — Period Of Invasions**

Dynasties Twenty-one through Thirty

Egypt invaded by the Lybians, Assyrians, Sudanese, Persians, and Alexander the Great. Alexander's general, Ptolemy succeeds as ruler of the nation. After his death his descendants continued to rule Egypt until the death of Cleopatra in 30 A.D. Rome made Egypt a province at Cleopatra's death and created great poverty and food shortages by its relentless demands for grain.

Egypt was a nation that welcomed early missionaries. The Bishop of Alexandria became one of the four most important authorities in the early church (along with Rome, Jerusalem, and Constantinople). Clement, Origen, and Athanasius were associated with one of the most important early centers of theological learning in Alexandria.

In 642 A.D.   Egypt became one of the first countries conquered by the rising forces of Islam